MW01193418

Breathe

Poetic Words of Love and Passion

By
P.D. Bates

when you have given to me
everything you have
i pull you into the warmth
of my arms
your body bruised and naked
and soaked
from the violence
of our love
and you rest your head
on my chest
close your tired eyes
and fall asleep to my breath
as i stroke your hair
with gentle fingers
and quietly adore you

you feel my warm breath
between your thighs
and shudder
as the tip of my tongue
finds you

curl into me
my love
and i will hold you
in the quiet strength
of my arms
and kiss the hot breath
on your lips

i feel the heat of you
against my lips
as gently
i brush away your hair
with the back of my fingers
and kiss your neck
your skin exhaling a wild
untamed fragrance
as you fall into me
like a soft whimper

with your head in my lap
my fingers stroke calm
through your hair
and the demons of the day
run in fear
of this love of ours

bared and beautiful
you part for me
and my eyes gently stroke
the soft skin
along the inside
of your thigh
as you arch and ache
to be taken
impatient for my heavy hands
to mark and claim
and ravage
to the point of ruin

the room is saturated
with the scent
of our intimacy

your body screams
silently
as my mouth finds you helpless
my lips
leaving a moist trail
along your inner thigh
your back arching
fists gripping
and ripping at sheets
while my wet tongue
soft and hot
presses slow circles
on your smouldering skin
unravelling you at the seams
before finally
lips taste lips
and you become
the most beautiful devastation

my kiss
on the delicate sculpture
of your lips
soft
then hard
then fierce

i take you
and it's not gentle
yet you've never known
such passion
never felt
such love

your hair lifted high
a tangle of midnight
in my grip
exposing the soft delicate skin
of your neck
screaming for my touch
for my bite

my fingers know you
in darkness

the buttons
of your summer dress
fly through the air
hitting the floor
like raindrops
as i unleash my hunger
upon you
tearing at your seams
with hands and teeth
your body
sighing with relief

watching you walk
the way you move for me
the smooth hypnotic slide
of your hips
slicing through the air
as my eyes
unclothe you

my lips and teeth
drag across your skin
and i delight
at the violent storm that rages
within the fluidity
of your body's response
as i destroy every last bit
of your sanity
with my dangerous mouth

my mouth presses
into the nectar
of your kiss
and your lips part
as i slide my tongue inside
the drum and bass beat
of my heart
thumping against your chest
as the weight of my body
pushes you harder
against the wall

together
is such a beautiful place
to be

my lips cover
every delicious inch of you
slowing down in the places
where you sigh

i kiss your shoulder
then softly whisper the truth
in your ear
that nothing about this
is going to be gentle

my love
you are the air
i breathe

i kiss the warmth
of your mouth
and feel the gentle softness
of your skin
beneath my fingertips
as they journey
along your parted thighs
to drown
within the warm melt of you

how you long
to shatter
beneath the weight
of my love

i tie you in knots
with a string
of filthy whispers

with lips and fingers
i make music of you

on white linen sheets
saturated with love
i hold you in my arms
and spill gentle whispers
into the nape of your neck
inhaling your secrets
as my lips press
upon warm scented skin
telling you everything
you could ever want to hear

i slide in slow
and you feel the warmth
of my love
deep in your bones

my hands
searched and found
and took
everything they wanted
from you

my lips brush
along the gentle curve
of your shoulder
covering your skin
with a warm veil
of whispers

there is destruction
on my lips
and i'm going to kiss you
everywhere

my fingers claw
the soft warm silk
of your skin
as i slide in deeper
penetrating you
with my hunger

i close my eyes
enjoying the heat
of your body
as i hold you
breathing in your scent
and feeling the caress
of your hair
against my lips

your lips
a seductive shade
of ravished red

i take your breath away
with a kiss
then take everything else

my fingertips on your skin
every touch
an unhurried whisper

i kiss your mouth
and finally we breathe

i wake
with a gnawing ache
that is
your absence

i count your heart
amongst my treasures

the journey of my lips
as they learn your secrets

when at last i hold you
in my arms
all the miles of separation
are finally reduced
to the heat
between skin
and the breath
between lips

the touch of my lips
on your skin
brands you
with a burning reminder
that you are mine

drowning your whimpers
with the thunder
of my body

i part your thighs
and slice you open
with my tongue

suddenly
i pin you to the wall
and the tenderness is gone
my kisses change
as do my eyes
and my voice
and my urgency

my mouth explores you
and tastes you
claiming you with lips
and tongue and teeth
and breath
until there's nothing
left for me to know

i hold you close
close enough for your heat
to become lost in mine

whispering my warm breath
on the soft silky skin
just above
your torn stocking tops

your body
clothed in moonlight
and marked
with love

you bite hard
on your bottom lip
to pull back the moans
but your body betrays you
as my fingertips
leave a trail of sparks
on your skin

between your thighs
you feel me
though i haven't touched you
not yet

my hand finds yours
and gives it a reassuring squeeze
and it feels so intimate
so special
as if this small gesture
belongs only to us

your skin listens
intently
as my fingers whisper
up your thigh

you lie there
so beautifully broken
and i kiss you
and breathe love's warmth
against your lips

i watch
the rising blush
in your cheeks
as my fingers
corrupt you

you slip
through my fingers
like silk sheets

i part your thighs
and you spill
your deepest secrets
onto my fingers

long after you leave
your imprint lingers
on my heart

i pull at the threads
that unravel you

the chaos
created by my lips
upon yours

my fingers
tangled in your hair
tugging hard
your head drawn back
throat exposed
my lips branding you
with a blistering kiss
claiming you

there's nothing gentle
in the way i kiss you

these endless moments
we make

my fingerprints
burnt into the soft skin
of your inner thighs

feel my thoughts
running all over you

i take you
in my arms
holding you
to my warmth
shrouding you
in my darkness
and bathing you
in all i am

this beautiful
brutal love
of ours

my world
would be painfully
incomplete
without you

whispers that soak
through your skin
and come to rest
between your thighs

hush my darling
this is just the beginning

one kiss
of your opium lips
and i was lost
forever

even when i'm gone
i remain with you
and you feel me
inside you
around you
holding you
touching you
filling you
saturating you

your body screams
as i tear you apart
and show you
how much i love you

goosebumps pop
on your skin
as my lips
touch the soft curve
of your shoulder
and my fingers
feel their way
down each notch
of your spine

your pleading fingers
rake down my back
as i force myself
deeper inside you

you hold my world
in your eyes

close your eyes
and feel the gentle brush
of my midnight whispers
in your hair

my fingers
on the zipper
of your little black dress
the pin
of a hand grenade
waiting for the pull

kisses like bullets
ricocheting
between lips and skin

a whisper of silk
across goosebumped skin

my hand gently brushes
against your thigh
and you burst into flames

our skin
drips with sweat
as we lie together
on slaughtered sheets
and crawl
into one another
naked and locked
in some perfect
human puzzle

not a word
passes your lips
as i pin you
against the wall
but your eyes say
"conquer me"

kissing you
where my fingers have been

i wrap you in my arms
and hold you
and fuck you
and love you
beneath the soft blanket
of a black sky

we kiss
and it's like fireworks
our lips
singed with fire

my fingers gently sweep
a whisper of hair
away from your neck
baring your skin
to the danger of my mouth

i kiss your thighs
igniting your skin
with warm breath
until you melt
onto my lips

my fingertips
on your fevered skin
every touch
a whisper of intent

i kiss your throat
and feel the throb of pulse
beneath the silken heat
of your skin

you change the way
my heart beats

i watch the beauty
of your ravaged body
and breathe in the scent
of your exhaustion
as you finally let go
and fall asleep
in the warm river
of my arms

i whisper
what i'm going to do to you
and you bite your lip
so hard it bleeds

i take you
to dark places
and make you
feel beautiful

exploring your depths
with the tip of my tongue

you are the madness
i live for

pinning you
against the wall
my hands shred
and rip
and tear at cloth
exposing you
to my darkness

lips pressed
in a kiss
that stops time

i see you in a way
that no one else does
i touch you in a way
that no one else can

i slip my tongue
inside you
and you know
this is going to be
a most delicious death

sheets gripped
in white knuckled hands
holding on
before letting go

your fuck-me
crimson lipstick
stains the soiled
white cotton sheets
where you met
your ruin

my fingers kiss
your velvety layers
spreading you open
like a butterfly

you contort
beneath my fingers
and the sound
of every one of your seams
ripping at once
inches up
from between your thighs

lips sliced apart
by my switch-blade tongue

in you
i have found
the most beautiful
of places

my gaze touches you
like soft fingertips
as my eyes take in
your beauty

i gaze along
the raw expanse
of your dark
irresistible beauty
my eyes marking
every spot
that my mouth
will devour

my whispers
tangle you in knots
so my fingers
can unravel you

i kiss your neck
and breathe you in
inhaling deeply
so i can carry you
inside of me

the slow dance
of soft fingertips
over slick wet velvet
inflaming
your incendiary needs
as you gently weep
down your thighs

dangerous hands
that lie to you
setting fire to your skin
and promising
you'll recover

i part your thighs
and taste you
licking the softened flesh
of your sighs
and savouring the glide
of wet silk
warm and naked
across my tongue

beneath the storm
of my body
you are set free

our bodies tangled
in twisted sheets
lips pressed in a kiss
that tastes like forever
we breathe
each other's breath
and glimpse heaven

the rasp
of silk stockings
along heated thighs
high voltage arcing
leaping across your flesh
as you prepare for the danger
of my touch

your hips
in my hands
like i'm clenching
fire

you sigh
against my fingertips
and whisper
'please break me'

what exquisite torment
it is
to love like this

heated whispers
that tickle your neck
then descend
down the arch of your spine
and settle
between your thighs

my finger
softly tracing your mouth
writing my name
on your tingling lips

your body
hums with desire
as my hands
show you no mercy

consuming you
one slow lick
at a time

you're torn apart
beneath the twist
of my tongue

my touch
against your skin
our mouths
drinking each other's lust
hands seizing the moment
whispers melting into screams
tenderness
madness
love

your hands clutch
at anything you can hold
as i fuck you hard
every inch
every throb
every thrust
reminding you
who you belong to

i undress you
leaving my fingerprints
everywhere

my hand
slides up your thigh
and my fingers assault
your slick greedy velvet
reducing you
to a liquid ache

there is no end
to where you
meet me

i slide another finger
inside you
and watch you crumble

as your sweat
slowly cools on my skin
my fingertips
gently trace
the marks of ownership
that colour your body

stillness
leaves your body
replaced by the slow rhythm
of arousal
as my mouth settles
on your clit
a small jewel
amid butterfly petals

a fuck
like a knife fight

opiate whispers
parting your thighs

flames licking
the back of your thighs
as you feel the fire
in my touch

you move
seamlessly
through every thought
in my head

i look down at you
and spare a moment
to consider
just how your body
will open
and surrender
and bruise
as i violently fuck you

your body arches
and aches
from this dance
of tenderness
and brutality

sparks flying everywhere
as our lips collide

as you part
your trembling thighs
let your fingers
be my lips and tongue

when i've taken
all you have to give
i hold you
pressing you to the warmth
of my skin
and leave you to drift
and wonder
at the beauty of this moment
and this place of ours

you close your eyes
and release a whispered sigh
as i gently lick the wet trail
running down the inside
of your thigh

the softness
your face brings
to my hands

i wrap around you
gently but firmly
and you become lost
and tangled
within me

i move your hair aside
and kiss your neck
with whispered lips
inhaling the sweet breath
of your skin
as you arch into me
and slowly melt

as the door
closes behind us
your mouth opens
to speak
and i claim it with a kiss
pinning your arms
behind your back
as i bite into the plump
of your lower lip

the night revolves
around our hunger

the whispered touch
of fingertips
that reach
every shadowy corner
of your soul

i hear the catch
in your breath
as my mouth
discovers you

you whimper
at my feet
as i lick my fingers
clean of you

my wet tongue
gently traces the outside
of your lips
as i pinch your nipple
between my fingers
and inhale
the deep aching need
in your breath

fingers searching
scents lingering
breaths whispering
tongues finding

your boundaries
are my kingdom

as our eyes meet
from across the room
i know
you can almost feel me
almost taste
the claiming kiss
i'll press
against your eager lips

you ache
to unfurl again
beneath the torment
of fingertips

holding you
to the warmth
of my skin
like i would never
let go

you drop to your knees
so i can feed you

i watch your body writhe
in the agony
of desire
as my lips caress your skin
and scorch my love
into you

hungrily we dance
inside one another

i bite you
as you cum

the tease
the chase
the capture
the rapture

held in place
by my growl

trails of flames
lick across the soft skin
of your inner thigh
as my fingertips
brand you
with their white hot
possession

you keep alive
this burning flame
inside my heart

i pin you down
and thrust inside you
and you feel me
raw and hard and deep
feel my hunger
as i unleash my savagery
upon you

you hear the groan
from deep inside my throat
as i penetrate yours

just a brush
of my lips
over your skin
and it's wildfire

my fingers
whisper and growl
across your skin

from across
the crowded room
my predatory eyes
lock on yours
and you're mine
instantly
instinctively

your lips
bruised by my mouth
and forced apart
by the violence
of my tongue

my hands
are aimless
when they're not
taking you

my fingers glide
across your heated skin
with a hungry purpose

merciless fingers
that reduce you to ruins

my fingertips
gently brush
across your breasts
and a wash
of tiny goosebumps
spread across your skin
infinite and beautiful

i am both your destruction
and your resurrection

my hands leave you
ignited
and devastated
broken
and beautiful

slowly you drip
like honey
on simmering heat

my lips
are at first tender
then demanding
as they press
and open
and possess

i unfurl you
with my tongue
petal by petal

you tremble
for deliverance
as i grip you by the hair
bite hard on your lip
and let my fingers
whisper along the inside
of your thigh

i touch your skin
and it feels
like there's fire
dancing
between my fingers

my fingers
trace gentle swirls
over the tender spread
of your thighs
feeling the marks
of ownership
left by my teeth

your eyes
so creamily seductive

seducing you
with opiate whispers

my hand
slips between your thighs
as i kiss you deeply
and remind you
i always take
what is mine

my body
speaks to yours
in whispers
of tenderness
and screams
of violence

you whimper
as my tongue
creates a wet trail
up your inner thigh
deliciously
agonisingly close
to where you so desperately
need it

a touch of my lips
on your skin
brands you
with a permanent
scar of me
a burning reminder
that you're mine

taste me
when you bite your lip

you tremble
beneath my body
and cling to me
as if i'm the one
who will save you

i hold your breath
as i slide inside you

you lose the power
to breathe
without my hands
around your throat

my tongue
plays at the edges
of your sanity
tormenting you
as you writhe and squirm
and barely remember
to breathe

i press you
against the wall
and there is no room
for words
or thoughts
or anything but my fingers
finding ways
to open you

when i'm done with you
you feel the lingering ache
in your body
for days
a persistent reminder
that you are loved
and you belong

i kiss you
and slide my hand
between your legs
a faint smile
weaving its way
across your lips
as i whisper
'that's mine'🛡

lying across my lap
i stroke your midnight hair
with gentle fingers
and tell you
how i'd rather die
than lose you

i protect you
from everyone
except me

in my arms
i hold you
in my heart
i keep you

you are
my morphine

i run my tongue
across the crimson blush
of your plump bottom lip
then gently suck it
into my mouth
feeling the exhale
of your warm liquid sigh
as my teeth sink
into the soft ripe fruit
of your flesh

my heavy hands
pin your delicate wrists
to the wall
as the violent passion
of my kiss
claims your hungry lips
in a bruising storm
pulling the breath
from your lungs

soft mouth
on warm skin
kissing a trail
of sonnets
across your beautiful
contours

fingers curled
in the tangle of your hair
my breath
hot on your neck
you feel my granite growl
against the soft silk
of your skin
as i fuck you
pressing deep
into your delicate delicious flesh
whilst planets collide
and explode around us

i hear
your lip bite moans
as my fingers
slowly unravel you
feeling the gentle fraying
of each
and every thread

i kiss your beautiful
chaotic mouth
and feel a stampede
inside my heart

you feel the palms of my hands
on your hips
burning
through the thin cotton
of your summer dress
as i pull you towards me
towards the fierce thrust
of my hunger

under a chandelier
of moonlight
i kiss your wrist
and feel the life of you
beating against my lips

the warmth
of my body
seeping into yours
my quiet fingers
moving through your hair
curling it
behind your ear
as i press my lips
to the moist exhale
of your mouth
and fuck you
so deliciously slow

you know my hands
and the earthquakes
they create

my soft tongue
flicking
at your hot skin
tasting your flavours

i feel your tiny shudder
as my warm breath
spreads the threads of hair
on the nape of your neck
and my gentle bite
reminds you you're mine

you look
so beautiful
covered
in my words

we lie together
exhausted and at peace
in the aftermath of our love
the white cotton sheets
from our war-torn bed
creased around bodies
sticky from sweat
and cum
the tickle of your hair
against my lips
as you nuzzle into the crook
of my neck
drinking my scent

my lips blaze
with a heat that can only
be quenched
by your decadent flesh

a touching of fingertips
lips and tongues
melding us together
as we feel everything
and hear nothing

show me your scars
show me where my lips
burnt your skin

not so gently
my mouth finds you

my fingertips
holding flames
that burn
with every light brush
and rough touch
of your skin

i can barely remember
when you became part of me
but I feel you here
inside my heart
every moment
of every day

my lips will not stop
nor my fingers give in
until you are mine
completely

your body sighs
as it feels the absence
of my hands

my mouth on yours
pulling the breath
from your lungs
as you give me your soul

pushed against the wall
seduced
by my mouth
and fingertips
abused and licked
into reckless surrender

you dance for me
your beauty
bathed in the dim light
your hips
casting spells
as they move
your eyes seductive
and dangerous

beneath my hands
i feel the storm
of your undoing

if i could just hold you
closer

this love of ours
both beautiful and fearsome
like a flame
that warms our cheeks
with its glow
and burns our lips
when we kiss

after the violence
of our love
my fingers
gently brush back the hair
from your face
and i kiss you
feeling the soft heat
of your smile
play on my lips

i bury myself
deep inside you
and you feel claimed
and lost
and hungry
and filled

i lift aside the cloth
that separates
my hungry mouth
from your skin
and trace delicious
lines of fire
across your thighs
with my lips

you stand quite still
as i undress you
my possessive hands
stripping you
of your innocence

i kiss your eyes
as you sleep
to make sure
i'm in your dreams

i feel the sigh
in your soul
as my soft lips
whisper against
your tired skin
and i wrap you
in the peace
and the safety
of my arms

i measure
the moments
of your absence
in heartbeats

close your eyes
bury yourself in me
and understand
that i love you
endlessly
you are my breath
my world
my life

i know
the darkest parts
of you
and i find them
so beautiful

i have your heart
and you have mine

i kiss you urgently
the way
you kiss someone
you've missed terribly
every day

with dangerous eyes
i watch you
as you slowly
and seductively
undress before me
daring me
with each gentle sway
of your body

i part you
and join us

you gently
run your fingers
across the delicious
bite marks
that stain your skin
feeling like the most
treasured of prey

the scent
of desire
the taste
of lust
the stirring
of passion
the touch
of madness

my fingers
leave you
so beautifully
undone

close your eyes
and fall into me

i wake you
with the soft stroke
of fingertips
gliding across your skin
with the fluidity
of gentle waters
lapping at your
naked beauty

i see you
wherever I look

you lay exhausted
in a twist of sheets
wrists bound
and pulled tight
above your head
your body
clothed in moonlight
and marked with love

i graze your shoulder
with my teeth
a mere whisper
of sensation
but i feel the shudder
that ripples across your skin
like an electric shock

my hand
slides between your legs
forcing them apart
and my fingers
feel the heat inside of you
like a fire
that's been simmering
all day

that first time
i pinned your arms
behind you
pushed you
against the wall
and crushed your lips
with mine
you knew
you were lost forever

captured
by my eyes
devoured
by my passion

to surrender
and to be taken
to give
and to be given
to love
and to be loved

i lift your chin
and our eyes gently touch

your hair rests gently
on your shoulders
hiding the bite marks
on the nape of your neck
that secretly mark you
as mine

your arms pinned
your legs spread
your breath stolen
your body taken

your scent lingers
upon my memory
keeping you with me
always

i wrap you
in my arms
and hold you
in my heart

soak inside my love
so i can know you completely
every touch
every sound
every pulse
every pore
every thought
every fear
everything

my lips hover
just a whisper away
from yours
my hands tangling
in your hair
nothing else matters
just this moment
just this kiss

this love of ours
where pain
and pleasure meet
where our bodies dance
and twine together
in raptures of flesh
where nothing exists
except us

pretty marks
all over your body
from our endless games

my tongue
leaves a small wet trail
along your throat
where i taste your skin
and you sigh
as i inhale you
and whisper
"you smell like mine"

with gentle lips
i kiss away your tears
take your trembling hand
in mine
and press it firmly
against my beating heart
"you are in there"

our eyes meet
and i slowly undress you
with my gaze
peeling away each layer
until you're completely
bared to me

my dangerous hands
on your dangerous curves

your wrists
locked behind you
restrained by nothing
but my voice

i calm your demons
with the gentle rise and fall
of my chest
and the steady beat
of my heart
as i hold you close to me
and quietly love you

i gently tuck
a stray lock of hair
behind your ear
and kiss your neck
feeling the faint throb
of your quickening pulse
against my lips

living without you
would feel like dying

your thighs part eagerly
and your back arches
as my fingers
slip inside your heat
and i whisper what my lips
and tongue are going to do

i'm going to
slowly seduce you
with my fingers
and my lips
and pull you
into my shadow
until you're completely
and irretrievably
lost in me

i love to hear
the harmonies
of your moans
and whimpers
as i tease and torment
your fragile body
with a delicious weave
of violence
and tenderness

don't be afraid
it's just love

my eyes
have already marked
all the places
on your body
where i'm going to
bite you

you fall apart
beneath me
as you feel
the slow scrape
of my wet tongue
along your inner thigh

we find madness
and sanity
in each other

we kiss and touch
until my lips
and the pads
of my fingertips
are raw from
possessing you

you are
my temptation
my unending
delirious
temptation

i cup your mouth
with my hand
to silence you
and your hot breath
rifles in quickening shots
against my palm
as my fingers
corrupt you

your breath
quivers
like a butterfly's
flapping wings
as i reduce you
to nothing
with a simple flick
of my tongue

i feel your body relax
as i tighten
my hold on you
my arms
surrounding you
squeezing you
painfully close to me

my hands
have a propensity
to utterly ruin you

i miss you
like i'd miss breathing

nothing about us
is ordinary

how perfectly
we fit

Made in the USA
Monee, IL
23 October 2020